# LIFE STORIES

# GEORGE WASHINGTON

Gillian Gosman

**PowerKiDS** press™

New York

Published in 2011 by The Rosen Publishing Group, Inc.
29 East 21st Street, New York, NY 10010

First Edition

Editor: Jennifer Way
Book Design: Ashley Burrell and Erica Clendening

Photo Credits: Cover, pp. 12, 22 (top) © www.iStockphoto.com/Duncan Walker; cover (inset), pp. 7, 12–13 Photos.com/Thinkstock; pp. 4–5 © www.iStockphoto.com/Grafissimo; p. 6 MPI/Getty Images; pp. 8–9 Reverend Samuel Manning/Getty Images; pp. 10–11 Taxi/Getty Images; p. 11 (inset) Time Inc. Picture Collection/Time & Life Pictures/Getty Images; p. 14 © www.iStockphoto.com/Nicoolay; pp. 14–15, 18 iStockphoto/Thinkstock; p. 16 © www.iStockphoto.com/Andrea Gingerich; pp. 16–17, 22 (bottom) Stock Montage/Getty Images; p. 19 © www.iStockphoto.com/Pictore; pp. 20–21 © www.iStockphoto.com/Clay Cartwright; p. 20 (inset) Getty Images.

Library of Congress Cataloging-in-Publication Data

Gosman, Gillian.
 George Washington / by Gillian Gosman. — 1st ed.
    p. cm. — (Life stories)
 Includes index.
 ISBN 978-1-4488-2581-3 (library binding) — ISBN 978-1-4488-2751-0 (pbk.) —
 ISBN 978-1-4488-2752-7 (6-pack)
 1. Washington, George, 1732-1799—Juvenile literature. 2. Presidents—United States—
Biography—Juvenile literature. I. Title.
 E312.66.G67 2011
 973.4'1092—dc22
 [B]
                                    2010032257

Manufactured in the United States of America

CPSIA Compliance Information: Batch #WW11PK: For Further Information contact Rosen Publishing, New York, New York at 1-800-237-9932

# CONTENTS

# Meet George Washington

George Washington was an **explorer**, a soldier, a farmer, and a president. He led U.S. forces in the **American Revolution**. He also helped write the **Constitution**. He was elected the first president of the United States.

George Washington played a big part in the formation of the United States.

Washington was one of the most important people of his time. The United States is the country it is today thanks to George Washington.

# Young George

George Washington was born in Virginia in 1732. His family owned several large farms. At 16, George joined an **expedition** to make maps of the Shenandoah Valley.

This painting shows a battle scene from the French and Indian War. The war lasted from 1754 until 1763.

Washington was 6 feet 2 inches (1.9 m) tall. This was very tall for the time during which Washington lived.

In 1752, Washington joined the **militia**, where he was made an officer. He fought on the side of the British in the French and Indian War. He faced death more than once but proved himself a great soldier.

7

Washington grew up in **Colonial** America. The colonists were mostly British and European. One quarter of the people living in the colonies were African slaves. It was an exciting time for Washington to be an adventurer and a young soldier.

This map shows the 13 colonies that became the United States after the American Revolution.

In 1760, the largest Colonial town was Philadelphia, Pennsylvania. It had 25,000 people. This is Philadelphia's Independence Hall.

Towns were growing. Settlers were exploring new lands to the west. By the 1760s, people were beginning to talk about the colonies becoming **independent** from Britain.

# Taking His Place

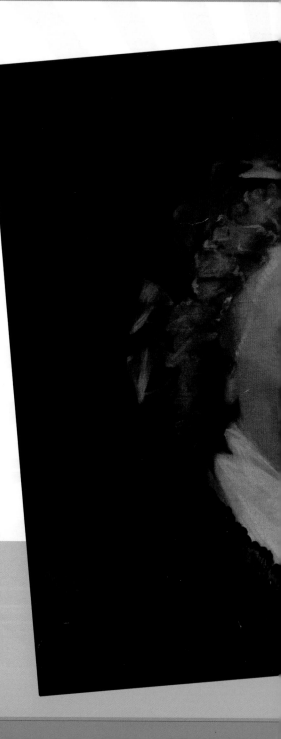

Washington left the militia in 1758. The next year he married Martha Dandridge Custis.

In 1775, Washington traveled to Philadelphia as a **delegate** to the Second Continental Congress. The Congress wanted the colonies to be independent from Britain.

Washington married Martha Dandridge Custis in 1759. This is a painting of her.

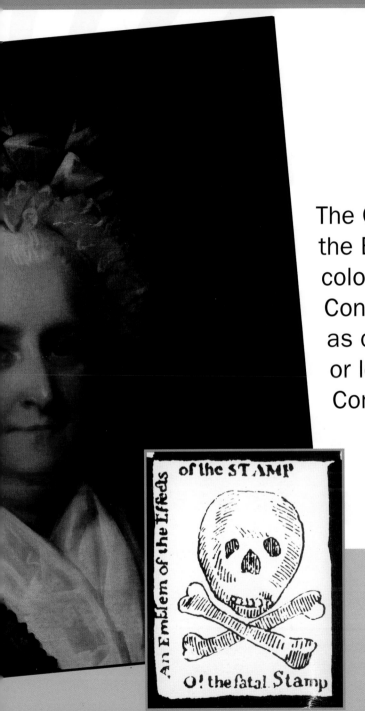

The Congress knew that the British would not let the colonies go without a fight. The Congress picked Washington as commander-in-chief, or leader, of the new Continental army.

This newspaper cartoon was made to show that colonists thought Britain's taxes on them were unfair.

# THE COMMANDER-IN-CHIEF

The American Revolution began in 1775. Washington and his men won important battles in the New Jersey towns of Trenton, Princeton, and Monmouth.

In 1781, Washington led his men to **victory** at the Battle

This picture shows Washington leading troops across the Delaware River to fight the Battle of Trenton in 1776.

This painting shows the British surrendering to Washington at Yorktown in 1781.

of Yorktown, in Virginia. The British surrendered. Britain agreed to give the American colonies their independence. The Treaty of Paris brought the American Revolution to an end in 1783.

# Writing the Constitution

After the American Revolution, the new states wrote the Articles of Confederation. It soon became clear that these articles were not strong enough to guide the new nation. In 1787, Washington led the delegates as

Washington led the delegates as they wrote the Constitution.

This is the Constitution. Each delegate had different ideas about how the Constitution would organize the government.

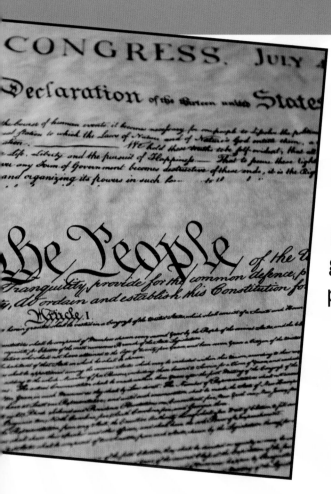

they wrote the Constitution of the United States.

The Constitution states the rights and freedoms granted to each citizen. It gives certain powers to each part of the government.

# THE FIRST PRESIDENT

By 1788, all the states had ratified, or accepted, the Constitution. The **Electoral College** picked Washington as the country's first president.

During Washington's presidency, there were wars going on in Europe.

Washington was sworn in as president at Federal Hall in New York City. Many people came to watch.

George Washington became the first president of the United States on April 30, 1789.

Washington felt it was best for the young United States to be neutral, or not to pick sides in the wars. Instead, he worked to bring the new states together as a strong, safe nation.

# LEAVING THE JOB

Washington served two terms as president of the United States. His second term ended in 1796. Washington believed that change was important for a **democratic** government. He did not want to become a lifetime ruler, like the kings of Europe.

Washington returned to Mount Vernon after he stepped down as president. His house still stands there today.

This picture of Washington is based on a 1796 painting by Gilbert Stuart.

Washington wrote a farewell letter to the nation when he stepped down as president. He told the people to work together to keep the young country strong.

After leaving office, Washington returned to Mount Vernon. He died there on December 14, 1799, from an **infection** in his throat. He was 76 years old.

Writers, politicians, and everyday citizens were saddened by his

Washington is honored in many ways. His face is on the quarter (bottom) and Mount Rushmore (top).

death. Many people wrote articles, speeches, and letters about Washington. Today, Washington is remembered as a great patriot and the Father of Our Country.

# TIMELINE

**February 22, 1732**

Washington is born in Virginia to Augustine and Mary Ball Washington.

**1754**

Washington is made a lieutenant colonel in the British army and is sent to fight in the French and Indian War.

**1775**

Washington is picked to be commander-in-chief of the Continental army.

**December 14, 1799**

Washington dies at Mount Vernon.

**April 30, 1789**

Washington is sworn in as the first president of the United States. He serves two terms and leaves office in 1796.

**October 19, 1781**

Washington defeats the British at the Battle of Yorktown.

# Glossary

**American Revolution** (uh-MER-uh-ken reh-vuh-LOO-shun) Battles that soldiers from the colonies fought against Britain for freedom, from 1775 to 1783.

**Colonial** (kuh-LOH-nee-ul) Having to do with the period of time when the United States was made of 13 colonies ruled by England.

**Constitution** (kon-stih-TOO-shun) The basic rules by which the United States is governed.

**delegate** (DEH-lih-get) A person acting for another person or a group of people.

**democratic** (deh-muh-KRA-tik) Having to do with a government that is run by the people who live under it.

**Electoral College** (ih-LEK-tuh-rul KO-lij) A group of people who pick the president based on who gets the most votes in a national election.

**expedition** (ek-spuh-DIH-shun) A trip for a special purpose.

**explorer** (ek-SPLOR-er) A person who travels and looks for new land.

**independent** (in-dih-PEN-dent) Free from the control of others.

**infection** (in-FEK-shun) A sickness caused by germs.

**militia** (muh-LIH-shuh) A group of people who are trained and ready to fight when needed.

**victory** (VIK-tuh-ree) The winning of a battle.

# Index

## A

American Revolution, 4, 12–14

## C

colonies, 8–11, 13
Constitution, 4, 15–16

## D

delegate(s), 10, 14

## E

Electoral College, 16

## F

farmer, 4
freedoms, 4, 15

## M

militia, 7, 10

## P

president, 4, 16, 18–19, 22

## R

rights, 4, 15

## S

soldier, 4, 7–8

## U

United States, 5, 15, 17–18, 22

## V

victory, 12
Virginia, 6, 13, 22

## W

women, 4

# Web Sites

Due to the changing nature of Internet links, PowerKids Press has developed an online list of Web sites related to the subject of this book. This site is updated regularly. Please use this link to access the list:
www.powerkidslinks.com/life/gwash/